To. OCTOBER 18TH

K B . L

DONGAKNUA

This is a letter containing the message that the artist wants to convey in the book *To. October 18th*. The composition of the following document consists of novels, music, and artwork. The contents of the following have a message that I would like to call my first love. The artist wants to produce a piece so that readers can experience art in a nice and relaxed way.

COLLECTION

© Photo by Hoonkoo lee

KB.L

ARTIST

Name : KB. L(kyabe. L)
Birth : 1986. 09. 29
Instagram : @ un_artiste_l

2003 Professional Boxing License
2005 Graduated from high school in Korea
2005 French Language Training
2007 Entrance to Versailles Vauxhall
2007 Gallery Boucle D'art Writers and Exhibitions
2008 La Maison Des Artists Registration
2021 Dongaknua Artist
2022 Representative of SJ Kunsthalle Seoul Group Exhibition
         Organizer
2022 Art Square Invitation Individual Exhibition
2022 Invited artist for the 2022 Goodbye Burnout Syndrome

작가명   : KB. L(꺄베. 엘)
생년월일   : 1986. 09. 29
인스타그램 : @ un_artiste_l

2007년 베르사유 보자르 입학
2007년 Gallery Boucle D'art 작가 and 전시
2008년 La Maison Des Artistes 등록
2011년 SJ Kunsthalle Seoul 단체전시 기획자 대표
2021년 동아크누아 소속 작가
2022년 아트스퀘어 초대 개인전
2022년 굿바이 번아웃 신드롬 초청 작가

Introduce the Artist 아티스트 소개

KB. L, who had never studied art as a child, left to study in France at the age of 18 with a vague idea of learning art. He started making his first paintings at the age of 19, and at that moment it became clear to him which path to take in life. After that, he worked harder than anyone in Paris to see the works of artists and immerse himself in artwork. With this determination, he managed to work on over two hundred canvases and over a thousand pencil sketches in about a year.

Seven months after starting painting in France, he became the first sponsored Korean artist at a small gallery in Paris at the age of 19. KB. L's art-work filled one wall of the gallery that brought him enormous prosperity, and as a result, patrons and artists of all levels started to interact with him and express a liking for his work. Additionally, art dealers and buyers flocked to purchase his creations and began assisting him in advancing his artistic career in Paris.

KB. L became officially acknowledged as a professional artist at the age of 20 after registering as an artist with La Maison Des Artistes, France's sole art association. KB. L rose to prominence as a young and gifted foreign artist in Paris, and this association is widely recognized and the goal of many painters working around Europe.

어린 시절 한 번도 예술을 배운 적 없었던 꺄베. 엘은 막연하게 예술을 배워야겠다는 생각만으로 만 18세 나이에 프랑스 유학을 떠났다. 그는 만 19세에 첫 그림을 그리게 되었고 평생 무엇을 해야 할지 그 순간 명확하게 깨우쳤다. 그 후로 파리에서 누구보다도 열심히 화가들의 작품들을 관람하고 미술 작업에 몰두했다. 그 결과 약 1년 동안 2백 점 이상의 캔버스 작업과 1천 장 이상의 연필 스케치 작업을 했다.

프랑스에서 그림을 시작한지 7개월 만에 꺄베. 엘은 19세의 나이로 파리의 작은 갤러리의 한국인 최초 후원작가가 되었다. 그에게 큰 행운을 가져다준 갤러리의 한쪽 벽에는 꺄베. 엘의 작품들이 가득히 전시되었고 그 이후 다양한 계층의 후원자와 예술가들이 그의 작품에 호감을 가지고 그와 교류하기 시작했다. 갤러리스트와 수집가들도 찾아와 그의 작품을 구매하거나 파리에서 지속적인 예술 활동을 할 수 있도록 많은 도움을 주기 시작했다.

꺄베. 엘은 만 20세 나이에 프랑스의 유일한 예술협회 La Maison Des Artistes의 작가 등록을 하여 정식 프로 아티스트로 인정을 받았다. 이 협회는 전 유럽에서 활동하는 많은 예술가들의 로망일 정도로 큰 인정을 받고 있는 협회이기에 그는 파리에서 젊고 유능한 외국 아티스트로 알려지게 되었다. 이후 한국에 돌아와 군 복무를 마치고 개인적인 예술 수련을 위해 조각과 설치 미술을 연구하며 예술관을 명확히 정리해 나가고 자신만의 작품세계를 만들기 시작했다.

© Photo by Hoonkoo lee

KB. L, qui n'avait jamais étudié l'art dans son enfance, part étudier en France à l'âge de 18 ans avec une vague idée d'apprendre l'art. Il a commencé à peindre à l'âge de 19 ans, et à ce moment-là, il savait claire-ment ce qu'il allait faire pour le reste de sa vie. Après cela, il a travaillé plus dur que quiconque à Paris pour voir les œuvres des peintres et s'immerger dans l'œuvre d'art. En conséquence, il a travaillé sur plus de 200 toiles et plus de 1000 croquis au crayon pendant environ un an.

Sept mois après avoir commencé à peindre en France, à l'âge de 19 ans, il devient le premier auteur piston-né coréen d'une petite galerie parisienne. Un mur de la galerie, qui lui a apporté une grande fortune, était plein d'œuvres de KB. L, et après cela, des mécènes et des artistes de différentes classes ont commencé à interagir avec lui avec un goût pour son travail. Des galeristes et des collectionneurs viennent également acheter ses oeuvres et commencent à l'aider à poursuivre sa carrière artistique à Paris. A 20 ans, KB. L s'in-scrit comme artiste à La Maison Des Artistes, seule association d'art en France, et est reconnu comme ar-tiste professionnel officiel. Cette association étant si reconnue qu'elle est la romance de nombreux artistes travaillant dans toute l'Europe, KB. L s'est fait connaître comme un jeune et talentueux artiste étranger à Paris. Après son retour en Corée, il a terminé son service militaire et a fait des recherches sur la sculpture et l'art de l'installation pour sa formation artistique personnelle, en organisant son point de vue artistique et en commençant à créer son propre monde artistique.

L-ART

까베. 엘은 그의 예술을 L-ART라 칭하고 "쓰다"라고 표현한다

K.B. L calls his art L-ART and expresses it as "writing"

In the beginning, human communication began using visuals rather than text. The artist realized that without art, there is no beginning, and the artwork of children started to make a lot of sense to him. Masters of art history and well-known contemporary artists agree that children's talent is difficult to match and that the best art is created by them when it is combined with creativity.

The work of children is authentic and truthful. This is as a result of the fact that they solely attempt to communicate their own point of view. In other terms, KB. L is attempting to tell his own story through his paintings. The concept of KB. L's L-ART is this young child's point of view.

His paintings contain the artist's life and his sincerity. His works simply express the message that the artist wants to tell as a form of art, and do not strive for flashy style or monetary gain. Perhaps this sincerity is why his works are so loved by European fans. One senses innocence in his art.

태초 인류의 소통은 글이 아닌 그림으로 시작이 되었다. 작가는 그림이 없다면 시작도 없는 것이라는 깨달음에 이르게 되었고 특별히 아이들의 작업물이 그에게 큰 의미로 다가오기 시작했다. 미술사 안의 대가들과 현시대의 유명 예술가들 역시 최고의 예술은 창의성이 동반된 아이들의 작업물이고 아이들의 재능은 그 무엇으로도 뛰어넘기 힘들다고 말한다.

아이들의 작업은 솔직하며 진심이 담겨 있다. 자신의 관점으로 생각하며 그 관점으로만 표현하려 하기 때문이다. 즉 그림을 통해 자신의 이야기를 하려 한다는 것이다. 까베. 엘의 L-ART의 개념이 바로 이러한 어린아이의 관점이다.

그의 그림에는 작가의 인생과 진심이 담겨져 있다. 그저 작가가 이야기하고 싶은 메시지를 예술 작품으로 표현할 뿐 멋을 부리거나 판매만을 위한 디자인을 하지 않는다는 것이다. 아마도 그러한 이유로 그의 작품이 유럽의 애호가들에게 많은 사랑을 받는지도 모른다. 순수함 그 자체가 느껴지기 때문이다.

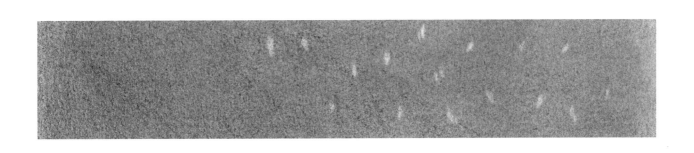

To. Octber 18th

To. Oct 18th 01, 2021 - canvas 33.3x24.2 in

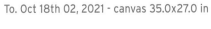

To. Oct 18th 02, 2021 - canvas 35.0x27.0 in

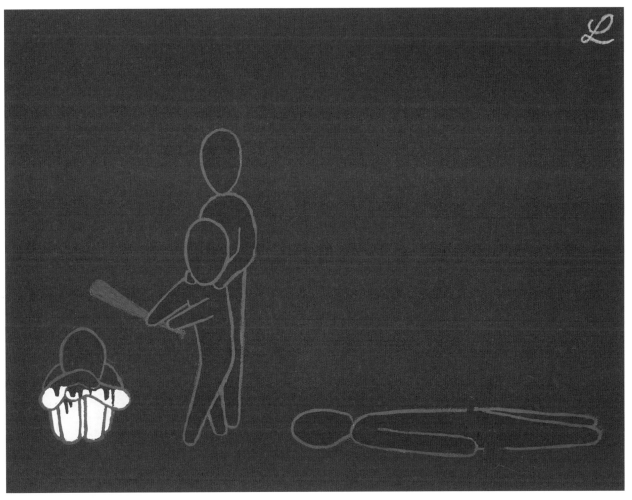

To. Oct 18th 03, 2021 - canvas 34.2x33.3 in

To. Oct 18th 04, 2021 - canvas 33.3x24.2 in

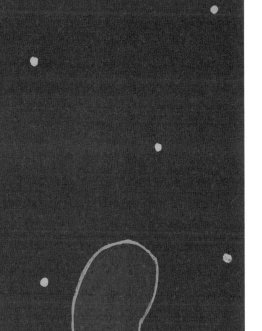

To. Oct 18th 05, 2021 - canvas 33.3x24.2 in

To. Oct 18th 06, 2021 - canvas 33.3x24.2 in

To. Oct 18th 07, 2021 - canvas 33.3x24.2 in

To. Oct 18th 08, 2021 - canvas 33.3x24.2 in

To. Oct 18th 09, 2021 - canvas 33.3x24.2 in

To. Oct 18th 10, 2021 - canvas 33.3x24.2 in

To. Oct 18th 11, 2021 - canvas 33.3x24.2 in

To. Oct 18th 12, 2021 - canvas 33.3x24.2 in

To. Oct 18th 13, 2021 - canvas 33.3x24.2 in

To. Oct 18th 14, 2021 - canvas 33.3x24.2 in

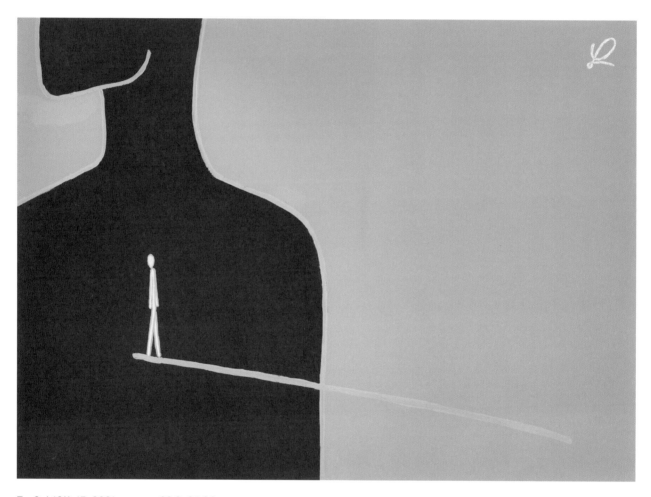

To. Oct 18th 15, 2021 - canvas 33.3x24.2 in

To. Oct 18th 16, 2021 - canvas 34.2x33.3 in

To. Oct 18th 17, 2021 - canvas 33.3x24.2 in

To. Oct 18th 18, 2021 - canvas 33.3x24.2 in

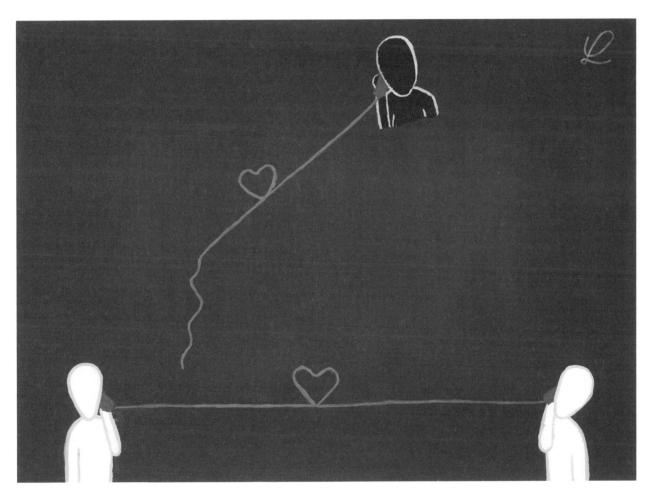

To. Oct 18th 19, 2021 - canvas 33.3x24.2 in

To. Oct 18th 20, 2021 - canvas 33.3x24.2 in

T O . O C T O B E R 1 8 T H

To. Oct 18th 21, 2021 - canvas 33.3x24.2 in

To. Oct 18th 22, 2021 - canvas 33.3x24.2 in

K Y A B E . L

To. Oct 18th 23, 2021 - canvas 34.2x33.3 in

To. Oct 18th 24, 2021 - canvas 33.3x24.2 in

To. Oct 18th 25, 2021 - canvas 33.3x24.2 in

To. Oct 18th 26, 2021 - canvas 33.3x24.2 in

To. Oct 18th 27, 2021 - canvas 33.3x24.2 in

To. Oct 18th 28, 2021 - canvas 33.3x24.2 in

To. Oct 18th 29, 2021 - canvas 33.3x24.2 in

To. Oct 18th 30, 2021 - canvas 33.3x24.2 in

To. Oct 18th 31, 2021 - canvas 33.3x24.2 in

To. Oct 18th 32, 2021 - canvas 33.3x24.2 in

Special Contents Of
To. Octber 18th

L – STORY

아티스트의 예술관을 바라볼 수 있는 통로

A way to see to creative viewpoint of the artist

The short story 'To October 18th' is a way to understand the artist's overall art world. Writer Sung-ji Yang has sincerely portrayed the story of life, love, and the world of art from the perspective of artist KB. L. This novel is also the short story debut of the writer who is working as a play screenwriter.

Short stories are also available in English. In order to convey the emotions that can be felt in Hangeul as it is, it was produced as a video by recording the work of KB. L and voice acting. It was translated into English by Kim Young-seong and voiced by Courtney Alexandria Garcia, a former American announcer.

If you read novels and see the works of artist KB. L, you will broaden your understanding of the author and his work.

단편소설 '10월 18일에게'는 아티스트 꺄베. 엘의 전반적인 예술세계를 이해할 수 있는 통로이다. 양성지 작가는 꺄베.엘의 예술가로서 바라보는 인생, 사랑, 작품세계에 관한 이야기를 진솔하게 담아 내었다. 이 소설은 연극 시나리오 작가로 활동하는 작가의 단편소설 데뷔작이기도 하다.

단편소설은 영문으로도 만날 수 있다. 한글에서 느껴질 수 있는 감성을 그대로 전하기 위해 꺄베. 엘의 회화작품과 성우 녹음을 함께해 영상으로 제작되었다. 영문번역은 김영성, 성우는 미국 전직 아나운서 코틴(Courtney Alexandria Garcia)이 맡았다.

소설을 보고 아티스트 꺄베 엘의 작품을 본다면 작가와 작품에 대한 이해의 폭이 넓어지게 될 것이다.

| CREDIT |

Writer Yang Sung Ji
Translator Kim Yeongseong
Narrator Courtney Alexandria Garcia
Multimedai Bonseung Koo

Created by 동아크누아(DONGAKNUA)

10월 18일에게
Korean ver.

To. October 18th
English ver.

L - MUSIC

회화 작품에 영감을 받은 음악 앨범

A music album inspired by paintings

The album *'To October 18th'* is a song that contains nostalgia for first love. KB. L left behind a photo diary in which he communicated his thoughts and words that he was unable to say at the time since he did not know how to articulate his emotions. His narrative was turned into a song.

앨범 '10월 18일에게'는 첫사랑에 대한 그리움을 담은 음악이다. 그때는 표현 방법을 몰라 전해지 못했던 마음과 미처 할 수 없었던 말들을 매일 쓰는 일기처럼 그림으로 남겨 놓은 아티스트 까베 엘. 그의 이야기가 음악으로 재창조되었다.

Track 1.
To. October 18th

_____

Track 2.
To. October 18th
[Instrument ver.]

_____

| CREDIT |

Produced by Soyoung Joung
Directed by KB. L / Lee Kyu Young

Song by Yoon Ji Hye
Composed, Lyrics by Sin Jun Chul
Art Worked by KB. L

Created by 동아크누아(DONGAKNUA)

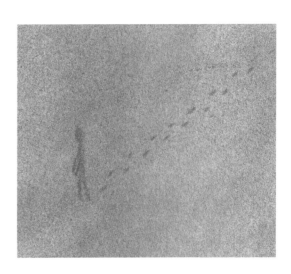

Epilogue

늘 참아야 했던 내 삶

늘 혼자 였었지

늘 내곁을 위로해준 내 방안 창문

창문 밖으로 보이는

너의 웃는 모습이

나에게는 늘 위로 였어

I always had to endure in my life
I was always alone
The window in my room
Always had my side

심한 장난으로

모두들 날 피할 때

너만 밝은 미소로

날 받아주었지

Your smile
Outside of the window
Always consoled my heart

When all avoided me because of pranks
Only you accepted me with a bright smile
I wanted to tell you how I felt
But it was not as easy
So, I started the art of drawing

마음을 말해주고 싶었어

그게 맘처럼 안되

그래서 시작했어 그리는 일

할수 있는게 그리는 일

또 그리고 그리다 보면

어느새 쌓여가는 나의 그림

매일 그렇게 편지를 보내

All I can do is draw
And the pictures pile up
As I continue to draw
My letters to you everyday

Artist KB. L
Publisher Soyoung Joung
DONGAKNUA, 2022
ISBN 979-11-960905-8-6 (03650)

601, 1, Segye-ro, Wonju-si,
Gangwon-do, Republic of Korea

https://www.dongaknuamusic.com

To. Oct. 18th

초판 1쇄 인쇄 2022년 09월 30일
초판 1쇄 발행 2022년 10월 18일

저   자 까베. 엘
발행인 정소영

불어번역 이하림
편집인 편집부 (정소영, 홍효민)

발행처 예술도서출판 동아크누아
출판등록 2017년 4월 28일 (제 979-11호)
주소 강원도 원주시 세계로 1 가든 식스 601호
전화 033-766-5010
팩스 02-6442-2901
홈페이지 www.dkmusiq.com

ⓒ 까베 엘
979-11-960905-8-6 (03650)
정가 20,000원

TO. OCTOBER 18TH

DONGAKNUA